CULTIVATING

Authenticity

IN A CURATED WORLD

Notes from a
Recovering
Perfectionist

MARGI REGEHR

Author's Note

This book was birthed while walking through a particularly hard season of heartache and disappointment. While I went through many motions of keeping up the usual appearances, my heart often felt like it was shattering into a million pieces. This internal struggle intensified at the onslaught of the 2020 COVID-19 pandemic and all the unknowns, sacrifices, and conflicts that came with it.

I lost my best friend of twenty years to cancer and—due to the pandemic—wasn't able to attend her funeral service.

Our family had to give up a once-in-a-lifetime trip I had researched and planned for six months—a trip we had gifted to our kids as a final hurrah before our oldest graduated and the kids started leaving the nest.

Another side effect of the pandemic was our work-from-home situation. I had just acclimatized to the quiet and freedom of having the kids in school after four and a half years of homeschooling—and suddenly, my kids and husband were in my space 24/7. This turned out to be the greatest gift down the road, and we bonded with each other through isolation, but it didn't happen overnight. Our marriage took a beating, and there were moments I wasn't sure if we'd make it.

I was also grieving the loss of some very dear friendships during this time. People who had walked beside us through some pivotal moments were no longer on speed dial.

As I mentioned, it was a season of intense heartache. It was a long year that brought anxiety, depression, and so much heaviness. As a highly sensitive and deeply empathic person, it was painful to watch our world—especially those I love—become aggressive and divisive. Nothing felt black and white anymore, and I found I didn't fully belong on either side of any debate.

I'll be the first to admit that writing a book—any book—is a massive undertaking for any recovering perfectionist. Writing a book about perfectionism is Next Level. I had so many stories to tell, but the uncertainty of the writing and publishing process had me stalled for years. As I neared my 39th birthday, I knew it was time to write for real and call myself a writer without cringing. It was time to set aside the critter that told me I was out of my league and just go for it, to take the risk and enjoy the ride.

I didn't want to tell anyone I'd begun writing an actual book. I figured if no one knew, then I couldn't let anyone down. I also couldn't win. It was the ultimate fail—not even daring to begin. This is how the ugliness of perfectionism has affected me. It tells me I can't fail if I don't begin, but in fact, the opposite is true—I fail because I'm too afraid to take that first step.

There's nothing so humbling as writing on a topic I have no "official" authority to speak on. I'm not a counsellor, life coach, or psychologist. I have no letters after my name. But I'm human, and therefore, I have the authority to speak about the human experience from the trenches. This book is a pure, raw human experience. I hope you learn from it. I hope you laugh, and cry, and feel... And heal.

I'm not here to tell you I have it all figured out. I'm a walking, breathing hot mess, but I am here, alive, and writing as if life depends on it. I wake up with words on my soul; I was called to create.

So, I created this book. If all it does is tell you to do that thing (you know the one), then it is worth it a thousand times over for me. And it will be the easiest coaching session you'll ever invest in.

Dedication

To my friend Pauline
1978–2020

I used to wonder what a "ride or die" friend was. The dictionary might as well have had your name listed. You were always my cheerleader, even if—especially if—you didn't understand why I made the choices I did. They were my decisions, and you loved me; that's all that mattered. You were the most loving, accepting, and supporting human I've ever known. I'm so grateful for the 20+ years of close friendship we had, for being able to raise our boys together, for all the belly laughs, for the soul talks, and the *Bachelor*-watching nights, for being goofy and strong and loyal and real. I miss you so much it physically hurts. But I know you'd be so proud of me for finishing this book.

Contents

On Perfectionism.

In my own journey of choosing authenticity in a world that is filled with curated newsfeeds and highlight reels, I've found perfectionism to be my nemesis.

Perfectionism isn't necessarily a bad thing. I'd like my surgeon—and my hairdresser—to be a perfectionist. On the positive side, perfectionism can guide us to do and be our best, whether we're writing an exam at school, working on a project for a client, or making a home-cooked meal. But there is a dark side to perfectionism that doesn't serve us. *Psychology Today* states that "Perfectionism is a trait that makes life an endless report card on accomplishments or looks. When healthy, it can be self-motivating and drive you to overcome adversity and achieve success. When unhealthy, it can be a fast and enduring track to unhappiness."

I think all of us have battled unhealthy perfectionism at some point, and never more so than in the social media influencer era. We are so used to consuming perfectly curated content online that we unconsciously measure our shortcomings with highly edited versions of other people. We only see what people put out there for us to see, and many people are simply not okay letting their unpolished sides catch daylight. This perpetuates a culture of perfection, or inauthenticity, both in appearance and performance.

I grew up in a conservative subculture where this was

especially true. As girls, we wore tightly braided hair and custom handmade dresses every time we stepped out our front door. We watched our words and how we walked, we "abstained from all appearance of evil" (1 Thessalonians 5:22 KJV). And while this was never rooted in ill intent, it built upon my core people-pleasing tendencies. I began to weigh everything I said and did against what the people around me would think. I would run scenarios in my mind of what other people would say or do if I wore this dress or combed my hair that way. How would they perceive me as a person if I bought these shoes and paired them with that sweater? Would I be more accepted if I took a more conservative approach to life? Did I want the approval of the "cool kids" or the church leadership? I became hyperaware of every move I made, and it was exhausting.

Although I didn't grow up with makeup or filters or Instagram or even cameras of any kind, there was still a strong sense that we must appear "put together," especially when guests were present. In my early years, my family babysat for a local teacher named Shirley who taught at the public school down the road. Before she arrived to pick up her daughter after school, we always did a quick cleaning, made sure the dishes were done, and put the laundry away. I remember Shirley admitting that she thought we'd achieved an unattainable level of perfection. From then on, my mom told us to leave the house as it was when Shirley came. In doing so, Mom taught me an important lesson. Portraying ourselves as "perfect" can create discomfort for the people we bump up against in life. Projecting a flawless front can hinder connection. My mom taught me to be authentic.

I always think about what Mom said that day because perfectionism has never served me. I recently mentioned to a couple of friends how I still constantly battle against per-fectionism. "Oh, I don't think you're a perfectionist at all!" was the reply. And I think I know what they meant.

I've become a lot more okay with having a less-than-perfectly-tidy house when they come over... but they will never see the battle I wage within myself to get to that place in my head every time I have guests over. I keep holding out hope that one day it will get easier.

Remember, a perfectionist will not necessarily have everything in order but will constantly feel "less than" if they haven't checked all the boxes.
What I have never feels like enough if my life is a report card on accomplishment or looks. But there is always a way to move past our base instincts and tendencies. It probably won't happen overnight, and I guarantee it won't all be easy. But it will be worth it.

Remember, loving your life > curating your life.
It takes a lot of time and energy to present a perfect front to the world. Release that pressure. Lean into the beauty that your life already has and learn to love it. Write down three to five things each day that you're grateful for. This can be as small as a ladybug on the windowsill or the smell of freshly brewed coffee. Practicing gratitude is the most effective path to loving your life.

Step away from social media.
While social media is a great tool for business, it can also feel like a lot to deal with on a personal level. It's okay to step away and take a breather without the constant influx of curated content. If it's affecting your mental health, just say no, even if temporarily. For most of 2020 and 2021, I worked as a social media manager for up to seven companies at a time. While I loved the work—both the creative and marketing aspects—I felt myself feeling really overwhelmed by the all-encompassing nature of the beast and made the decision to step away.

Remember, your life ≠ their life.
We each have our own priorities and goals, so the process is going to look different. It's easy to get distracted by others' holdings and activities, but their life has a different trajectory than yours. Their goals are not your goals. Keep your eyes on the

prize and learn to enjoy the journey, even when the pace is different from the pace of others.

"Perfectionism is the voice of the oppressor, the enemy of the people. It will keep you insane your whole life."

—Anne Lamott

On White Shoes.

I remember the first pair of new shoes I ever owned. I had just turned seven and was about to start grade one. Mom had taken me shopping, and although money was tight and brand-new clothing was rare, we found a pair of white canvas shoes covered in tiny, colourful pencils. I was so proud of those shoes. As the youngest of ten, most of my belongings were handed down, but these shoes were all mine. I rarely took them off, wearing them around the house up until school started. When we had guests, I paraded them around so they would get noticed. They were perfect.

Sometimes, I find I'm still parading around in those perfect white canvas shoes. I like showing off the curated parts of who I am—the new stuff—while the old, scuffed hand-me-downs are kicked into a closet with the door firmly closed. If you're honest, I think you probably would admit to this too. It's in our human nature to feel like we need to hide our stained and holey parts. We highlight the bright white canvas, bring attention to the pretty little pencils because we're proud of the new, pristine, cute parts. But the more people show only their shiny, flawless pieces, the more alone we all feel. Every time we face a seemingly insurmountable hurdle, we think that no one out there could possibly understand. That we could scream and no one would hear.

These are all lies. There is no struggle you or I can face that someone else can't relate to on some level. But, to cultivate authenticity, we need to practice raw vulnerability. We need to be willing to appear as our true messy and flawed selves, to share those scuffed and holey parts. Only then can we experience genuine connection. When I share my intimate struggles with depression, anxiety, unmet expectations, and grief—both online and off—I hear, "Thank you for being brave. I thought I was the only one. You've given me courage." All I did was strip away the filters and tell the truth. If that gives one person the courage to face another day, I will do it with joy.

In the age of social media, I no longer believe it's optional to be our true selves, even if it's hard. It's always going to feel vulnerable. But it's always going to be worth it. In our always-connected digital era, we are constantly bombarded with "proof" that everyone else's lives are amazing, beautiful, adventurous, and blessed.

If you spend any amount of time on a mindless social media scroll, you will likely feel as if you're not measuring up to some invisible bar. That's where you and I get the perfect opportunity to share the real and raw, admit the little struggles of marriage or parenting or family dysfunction. Obviously, we don't need to overshare, but I think it's important we give voice to the authentic life experience that I know we all have. I'm drawn to those voices on my feeds, and each time I see a post that is raw and authentic, I'm left with a glimmer of hope and a feeling of "I'm not the only one. I'm in good company."

Be real on social media.

There's a time and a place for professional photography and curated content, but it's important to keep it real too. You don't need to clean up your whole kitchen before showing the cookies you're baking with your daughter or wait for a perfect hair day to show up on a live video. Be real. Show up. Spread hope.

White shoes don't naturally stay white.

Brand-new white shoes are, obviously, white. But when

you've worn them around the block a time or two, they're going to be slightly dusty and gently scuffed. The more you use and love them, the more worn they'll start to look. No one expects you to still look like you're twelve. You've lived some life; you have the laugh lines and stretch marks to show for it. Wear makeup if you like, play around with filters for fun if you want. But just remember, you are not flawed and you are not shameful if your body shows a little wear and tear. Think of each grey hair and wrinkle as a passport stamp from a life well lived.

"Perfectionism is internalized oppression."

–Gloria Steinem

On Education.

As a kid, I loved everything about school. I loved the beginning of the year, when we flipped the calendars over to September, the air turned crisp, and I headed off to our little private country school with new pencils and notebooks tucked into my blue-and-white floral cotton bookbag. I will never forget that first day of grade one, proudly sporting those white shoes and a blue dress with an all-over mushroom print. I couldn't be happier; I'd watched my siblings head off to school, one by one, and couldn't wait for my turn. I spent a lot of my time playing "teacher" with all my stuffed animals lined up in front of me. Nothing made me happier than that dark little converted storage room in the basement. I had my own teacher desk, a wall-mounted chalkboard, and a class that could never take their eyes off me.

My love for school and books—and teaching my stuffed animals—really was no surprise as my mom had been a substitute teacher in the public system, and seven of my nine siblings had all taught in small private schools within our Mennonite communities.

As a young girl in my sheltered rural community, I never aspired to a higher education or a career. My only goals involved graduating from grade nine (the highest grade offered), then getting married as young as possible and having babies. I wouldn't say it was all the result of my upbringing as I adored babies and often dreamed of my own home. Even though I was the youngest child, my oldest nephew was born a year after me, so there were always babies around. I had no lofty goals of becoming a doctor or lawyer or airline pilot; those ideas simply were never discussed or dreamed about. We lived a simple life and didn't see a high-paying career as the ultimate success. We were hardworking children of farmers, mechanics, carpenters, electricians. If by some chance I didn't marry young, I would pursue a career in nursing or teaching.

It was only once I'd been married for fourteen years and had four children, ages 11 and under, that I began to desire building something that was all mine. The entrepreneurial bug bit, and my professional organizing business was created. It was at a birthday party in February 2016 that I first heard the term "professional organizer." The girl I had just met was trying to explain what her business was, and I thought there couldn't be a dreamier job. It would be eight months before I would put that dream into action and create FreeSpace Professional Organizing. I was a natural-born organizer and enjoyed helping people find freedom and create margin within their homes. For over three years, I helped clients lose clutter and get organized. I embraced each household where they were at and created systems that worked for them. There were no expectations of perfection or unattainable one-size-fits-all methods. I forged some beautiful friendships with these clients and learned many valuable lessons as I grew my business.

When our world changed in the spring of 2020, I chose to pivot so that I could work from home and be present for my kids as they moved to online schooling. I missed the organizing, but I used those same skills as well as an eye for design and a love of writing to start social media marketing, which morphed into freelance writing and editing. My experience as an organizer helped me keep my clients' files organized and their content posted on time.

I always thought I needed to follow a perfect path and have a high school diploma, or do some upgrading, then get a university degree to accomplish anything in life. But I sit here at age 39, with no high school education at all and no diploma in my hand, proudly holding my professional editing certificate from a local university. This prized piece of paper represents two years, one hundred hours of editing, more late nights than I can count, several deadlines pushed, and probably a few extra grey hairs.

I've finally realized that I have what it takes to do the work, whether it's a perfectly planned and executed journey through traditional education or not. It doesn't matter if I have certain qualifications such as a high school diploma or university degree. When I received my certificate in the mail, I sat in my car outside the post office for a few extra minutes before I drove away. Several tears snuck down my cheeks as I clutched the envelope. I felt exuberant. I'd achieved a dream that I never thought was possible.

I may still work on a degree at some point, but it will be for my own learning and growing and not to prove myself. For so much of my life, I've listened to a negative tape in my head that said, on repeat, "You're just an uneducated, uncultured Mennonite." I knew in my head that it was a bald-faced lie, but my heart hesitated. Because maybe I felt my value did lie in my education (or lack thereof).

It's so hard to be authentic when you don't feel confident in the beauty of who you were created to be. Does exterior validation feel good? Oh, yes. Having a university certificate on my wall feels amazing. But I know that leaning on that alone is shaky ground. Just as I was created to be sensitive and empathic, I was also created to thrive in my world of writing and creating and editing, with or without a traditional path of education. I can rest in this and step off the hamster wheel of "not enough."

You can too.

No matter what part of your life feels like you're on a path you didn't choose, rest in the truth that you were created in love to fill a place in this world that no one else can. Maybe you didn't have a supportive parent when you were growing up or the money to pursue your dreams. Maybe you got pregnant young or couldn't get pregnant when you desperately wanted to. Maybe the people you loved most died and the ones who hurt you stuck around. You are still loved, and the world still needs *you*, wherever you are right now.

Throw out the lies that say you're not equipped, that you're not perfect.

You have everything within you to be kind, compassionate, and authentic. And the world so desperately needs that right now. Someone out there, right now, needs to hear your story to know that they're not alone.

Take courage in knowing you don't need to have perfect beginnings.

"If you succeed at loving imperfect people, then it becomes plausible that somebody could love imperfect you.

—Bishop T. D. Jakes

On Marriage.

As I write this book, my husband and I are celebrating our 21st anniversary. It is bonkers that we've been married for that long. And yet some days/weeks/months it can feel like an eternity. Marriage is freaking hard. It is the hardest thing I have ever done or ever will do. Is it fulfilling and beautiful and the biggest blessing in my life? Absolutely!

But it is so, so hard. Anyone who tells you differently has been married for about five days or isn't being honest. Whenever you put two humans into the same space for an extended period, at some point that humanness is going to show. There will be conflict. There will be irritability and impatience and sometimes a hot spark of anger. Put the same two humans in the same space for eighteen months over a pandemic, attempting to live and work and parent and play in the same few square feet, and you'll quickly find the limits and raw edges.

We got married on a hot July day on the Saskatchewan prairies, eight short weeks after getting engaged and only nine months after we'd first laid eyes on each other. We never dated, and we only saw each other in person four times. In the culture we grew up in, dating simply wasn't a part of the process. Our marriage was not arranged, though. (We get asked that a lot!)

I had just turned 18 a month earlier. We met at a mutual friend's wedding in northern Alberta in the fall of 1999. I was hanging out with a bunch of young people at my cousin's home when this tall blond guy came down the stairs, and something changed in me the moment I laid eyes on him. I leaned over to my friend Kevin and asked, "Who... is THAT?"

"Oh, that's Jer," he replied. The Mennonite community is close-knit enough that I knew who he meant. I had been friends with this blond's sister Julie for a couple of years and had heard her talk about her brother, but I had never met him. That weekend I was never far from his side. Dating wasn't an option, hanging out together alone wasn't an option, but we could visit in groups, and we made the most of it. Conversation came easy. He was smart, funny, and made me feel like the most beautiful and interesting girl in the room. The next day as we were travelling home from the wedding, my carful of girls met his carful of guys at West Edmonton Mall. This mall is the second largest shopping mall in North America (second only to Mall of America) and contains an amusement park, complete with the world's tallest indoor roller coaster, the Mindbender. It was slightly unorthodox to meet other single youth in this environment without chaperones, and we caught a lot of heat for it later, but I had so much fun! I'd never been to any type of theme park, never rode a roller coaster, never fell in love... before that crisp day in October. Nine times, back-to-back, I rode that coaster, and my heart did a lot of loops that had nothing to do with the ride. I loved his muscular thighs encased in medium-wash Levi's, his dimples, his contagious laugh, his silky blond hair. He had zero fashion sense, but that was oddly compelling as well. I was smitten.

We parted ways, not knowing what the future would hold. I came home and my parents knew instantly something had happened. I often wonder if they wished they'd hung on to me... it was the one time they'd let me go to a wedding without them, and here I went and fell in love... with a guy from a much less conservative home than I was used to. We belonged to the same denomination but couldn't have been raised more differently within that framework. I was the youngest of ten; he was the oldest of four. My parents were of the same generation as his grandparents, so there was simply a different outlook on life. My mom was about to turn 46 when I was born; his mom was 22. His family was young, lively, progressive, while my family was reserved and conservative.

Over the next nine months, we found ways to communicate. I wasn't allowed to call boys, but I found a loophole and would call Julie, then ask to speak to her brother. When my parents heard me on the phone, they'd ask who I was speaking to. "Oh, I just phoned Julie," I'd say.

July 23, 2000, was our wedding day. Three hundred and eighty people celebrated with us, but I couldn't wait to leave and head off into the sunset with my new husband. We had never kissed and had only briefly held hands once, surreptitiously under my parents' dining table. I know that it could have all been overwhelming when physical contact is off limits and then suddenly it's open season, all in one day. But we loved each other, and I fully believed then, and still do now, that God brought us together and walked every step of the way with us. Our wedding night was not terrifying or weird or awful. It was beautiful. My husband was selfless and gentle and kind. He always has been, and he always will be. I don't take this blessing for granted.

I will not stop here and let you think it was all roses. Uh-uh. Connecting sexually has been a challenge for us the entire twenty-one years we've been together. Bring together two very different people with different libidos, throw in four kids in those first twelve years, add in the regular challenges of life and work, and it can be more than hard. Sometimes it can feel impossible. I've been grateful a million times over that we were both raised in homes where divorce wasn't a first option. Please don't hear me wrong, if there had been abuse or toxicity, divorce absolutely would have been recommended! But for us, it was the rubber band that kept us leaning back toward each other. It took so much hard work, and it still does! If I'm completely trans-parent, I will admit that 2020-2021 has been the very most difficult year for us as a couple, as I know it was for many couples. Divorce was mentioned. There is no one easy path through life, through parenting, through marriage. Divorce is hard. Marriage is hard. We pick our hard.

Instead of throwing away the twenty-one years we'd invested, we decided to grow. Both individually and together.

I went back to therapy, and Jer started taking personal development intensives online. I worked on numbing less through work, Netflix, and shopping. I'll let Jer tell his story on his own time, but I watched him start drinking less, working out consistently, connecting with our kids, and just being all around more present, more focused, more alive.

We'd done marriage counselling, and I still highly recommend it. But we didn't need to learn how to get along better. We've always known how to get along well. We genuinely enjoy each other's company, most of the time. We know how to be friends. We needed to learn how to get that passion back, and for that, we needed to focus on our own growth for a while.

We started booking intimate dates and being intentional with them.

It was often bumpy, and clumsy, and awkward. It's not a smooth transition to start talking about deeply intimate things when you've tried to avoid it for so long. There were—are—still tears, frustration, and impatience at times. But we're committed. I think that makes all the difference. You can feel stuck in a marriage, or parenting, or faith. But when you walk through the fire, face all the demons, and make the choice on the other side to stay, it undergirds everything. It's easy to commit when you're 18 and 20 and have yet to experience life, but making a commitment when you've been through a few fires together forges a rock-solid foundation.

There are a lot more wrinkles and pounds and silvery hairs between the two of us today, and those "new love" butterflies flutter a little less, but the love that has formed over twenty-one years is deeper and more profound than either of us could have imagined. We chose us. We continue to choose us. We choose letting Jesus lead our marriage and our home. For us, it has made all the difference.

On our eighteenth anniversary, I wrote this list of imperfect marriage tips, and it holds just as true today as it did then.

Laugh.

A lot. Laugh when you're grumpy, sick, or angry. Find someone who makes you laugh so hard you pee your pants. Because honestly? Life can be hard and sad and crazy and sometimes nothing makes it better besides a good hard laugh with your best friend.

Let it go.

Some things—okay, most things—can probably be released long before we want to. You know that "5 by 5 rule," if something won't matter five years from now, don't spend more than five minutes thinking about it? Yes, that.

Fight cai ly.

Seriously. Don't bring up those make-or-break issues after 10 p.m. Just don't. Even if you're both night owls. Discuss it early or put a pin in it until the next day. Occasionally, that issue that seemed so difficult when you were tired is not that big of a deal the next day.

Fight.

Period. We went through a (long) time where we didn't fight. We skirted around hard things and retreated into our silent caves until it was "safe" to come out. It was not a healthy place to be in. Learn how to fight and fight well. Have the hard conversations when you are able to speak calmly (take twenty minutes to cool down if needed) and not when in "fight or flight" mode.

Counselling is not for the weak.

Quite the opposite in fact, and a great idea to do before you feel the relationship is in trouble. My husband and I went to couples counselling as maintenance, and it was such a great experience. We take care of our cars with regular oil changes, consistently checking the tires, working to prevent problems, but somehow that concept is often lost when it comes to the most important things in our lives, relationships.

Turn toward instead of away.

This is one vital tool I took away from our counselling. The Gottman Institute did a six-year study on newlyweds and found "[a]t the six-year follow-up, couples that stayed married turned towards one another 86% of the time. Couples that had divorced averaged only 33% of the time." The secret is turning toward each other. This starts with paying attention. Recognize when your partner is making a "bid" for connection and respond in kind. Dr. John Gottman provides a "list of minor bids for emotional connection" on his website at: https://www.gottman.com/blog/turn-toward-instead-of-away/

Don't forget who you are.

Sometimes we get so busy being a couple/parent/business owner that we forget to feed the "me" that was before "us" or before kids. Sometimes spending a little time apart is healthy for the growth of a relationship, especially for the one who may be a little more introverted.

Have more sex.

Seriously, if you're married and committed to each other for life, find ways to express and explore sexually together. It's one of the best ways to stay fully connected in the chaos of raising a family and building a business (or two!).

Find things to do together.

Before we were married, we had everything in common. Ha. Then life and kids happened, and now we know we need to be more intentional in finding common ground. It's so worth it to find something that fills us both up. Maybe it's playing music together, hiking, or hey, even grocery shopping! My parents have been married for fifty-nine years, and every evening they sit together in their recliners and silently read their books, with the odd comment to each other. I think it's beautiful.

Be adventurous.

Find new things to try as a couple... it might be trying a new recipe or spending an afternoon at the gun range. It doesn't have to cost a ton of money but learn a new skill or experience something. Together.

Don't forget to date.

This is hard when you have younger kids and need to find a sitter, but it doesn't seem to get a lot easier when the kids are old enough to stay by themselves. I believe making it a top priority to get out by ourselves no matter what stage the kids are at will pay off in spades when the kids are all gone. I don't want to send off the last kid at 18 and look across the dinner table at a stranger.

Find that little thing.

We each have those small loves that don't look like a lot but can transform our day. For example, coffee is my love language. When my husband has to leave early in the morning, he leaves a steaming mug by my bed so I wake up to the smell of fresh coffee. It's such a little thing, but it's everything. It's one human telling another, "I care, I notice, I sacrifice, I love."

Create spiritual whitespace together.

White space in graphic design is the empty space surrounding the elements, enhancing their beauty and richness because there isn't clutter overpowering them. I believe that we all have a spiritual part of us that needs growth and space. For us, it has been attending church together, and I love that our home church allows us to drop off our littles in the kids centre before the band starts and we can fully focus on worship in the same space. As the kids grow older, they are choosing to stay in the service with us, and I crave that hour every week spent together.

Go camping.

You know those T-shirts you can buy that say something like "I'm sorry for what I said while you were trying to park the camper"? Nothing brings out the raw, unfiltered emotions like roughing it for a few nights. And despite the heated words that can come with the experience, I always feel like it bonds us all a bit more. The frustrations from setting up the camper, living in crowded quarters, getting chilled or overheated... But at the end of the day, it's a shared experience that brings us all closer together.

Volunteer together.

Nothing does the heart good like giving of ourselves for someone else, with no expectation of return. Doing this as a couple (or family) is just so important. Serve at a local soup kitchen, play music together at a church event, or usher at a live theatre event.

Say "The thing I love most about you is..."

This is a great one to do daily, whether or not you're "feeling it." It can be the tiniest thing, like "The thing I love most about you today is that dimple in your left cheek..." The important thing is that you do it.

See things from their point of view.

Probably the hardest, but in my experience, the most important. Some of the most infuriating things my spouse has done or said take on a whole new meaning when I put myself in his shoes. If I stop for a second before I open my mouth and imagine how it looks from his point of view, how much better will I react? I use this a lot in other relationships too. *If I reversed this situation, how would I feel?*

Say "I was wrong."

A tie for the hardest, this one will change your entire marriage (or any other relationship). Humility never goes out of style. Being humble enough to admit you were wrong and vocalize it can transform your relationship with not only your partner but your kids as well.

Apologizing well requires more than just "I'm sorry." Anyone can feel sorry about a situation, but to move forward, you need to take action. A great apology requires three steps:

1. Acknowledge your misstep. *"I forgot our lunch date."*
2. Apologize sincerely and simply. *"I apologize."*
3. Ask how you can make it right. *"Can we reschedule for dinner?"* or *"How can I make it up to you?"*

And remember, "the best apology is changed behavior." - Unknown

"The reason we struggle with insecurity is because we compare our behind-the-scenes with everyone else's highlight reel."

—Steven Furtick

On Parenting.

When we first get pregnant or adopt that sweet innocent child, we have an idea in our minds how it is going to go down. We often place our expectations on who our kids might become, and I doubt there is a parent alive who hasn't done this to some extent.

Our kids grow up in our homes with our influence, our training, our modelling... and they still develop an entirely unique personality, independent of who we think they should be.

I wrote the following blog post during a challenging time in parenting when reality wasn't matching up to expectations.

> *Sometimes we try to change you. Sometimes we grieve for the child you aren't.*
>
> *Sometimes we full-on cry because you are so much more amazing than the kid we dreamed of having. Because you are brave. You are okay being you even if it's not— especially if it's not—like all your peers. You are aware of your unique interests and abilities, and you desire to share them with the world. This chokes me up every time because you are so far ahead of where I was at your age.*

Sometimes we see how others look at you and we cry again. Because they don't know you. They see only what you aren't—the lack, not the fullness of your brilliant, intense, sensitive self. The "you" that still comes to my bedside at night, all long legs and arms, to wrap me in a goodnight hug.

Daily, I'm grateful. To our Creator, for gifting me with the children I never dreamed of having. For stretching my mind and heart and life to include you and all your amazing brilliance.

And to you, my child, for you are nothing like I'd imagined and so much more than I'd hoped.

It was an unspoken goal of mine—and many of my friends—that we would get married at 18. I had no plan past that, no idea of a life outside of mothering and homemaking. I was raised to believe the highest calling a woman could have was that of a wife and mother. I have always had a nurturing nature, I've always loved babies, and I don't disagree that being a mother is an incredibly important role. Before I was married, we discussed that we would wait two to three years to get pregnant and then have three or four beautiful, healthy babies. In my mind, this meant we would all live in a blissful pink fog forever after.

I was always a bit of a dreamer as I was growing up, and I never let reality get in the way of a good imagination. The thing is, I *did* meet a "tall, blond, and handsome" at age 18, fell in love at first sight, and *did* get married when I was two months shy of 19. We went on to have four beautiful, healthy children, perfectly spaced, just as planned. But there are a million jolts of reality within the mundane that my childhood dreaming didn't prepare me for. That pink fog faded quickly as colic, sleepless nights, and a loss of identity settled in.

One such jolt came when our second son, eight at the time, was diagnosed with ADHD. I remember a haze of grief, anger, and heavy sadness with the diagnosis. Even though my son has managed his ADHD well, it felt like a loss for me. The scrubbed and perfect family you see in staged photoshoots had been yanked away from me, and a very real and challenging version had replaced it. This version included my 8-year-old son curled up in the fetal position in the school's office because he couldn't deal with the overstimulation of the classroom setting. It involved my heart breaking into a million pieces because my son was struggling and I didn't know how to help him, but also—and this is so hard to admit—because I'd never prepared my heart for an "imperfect" child.

We didn't know where to turn for help with our twice-exceptional child (twice-exceptional refers to a child having a combined diagnosis of a behavioural disorder, such as ADHD, and giftedness). My husband and I only knew private education; we'd been raised to believe that public schools were substandard, and we were convinced the public system wouldn't be a fit for our family. Since public school was the only option in our small town with educational support for our son, we started looking at relocating. When our plans to move near an acclaimed private school in a nearby city fell through, we started homeschooling. It seemed like the ideal solution to our son's challenges. We could get him the best academics that were out there, hand-picked classical literature and hands-on learning with frequent trips to the local science centre and robotics classes, hiking and travelling, and acting in the local Badlands Passion Play. The whole of our world was suddenly educational, and I was lapping it up. I felt like I had this whole purpose suddenly, a way to make a difference in my kids' lives.

We homeschooled for over four years, and it went well for most of that time. I loved the time with the kids, and shockingly, I found they got along better. I found my oldest son bonding with my youngest daughter in ways they never would have if they had been at school every day. My precocious 6-year-old taught my 4-year-old how to read. Some days were really, really hard. Some days I taught a small human a new concept and rode the dopamine high for several days. But, as all good things do, it came to an end. In the fall of 2018, we started homeschooling for the fifth year.

About six weeks into the year, I started to feel an unease in my heart, and I told my husband, "I think the kids need to go to school and connect with their peers on a more consistent basis." My husband had been impressed with the same thoughts that week, and we knew it was a divine intervention. On November 1, we sent our "littles" off to public school for the first time outside of kindergarten. They were in grades three and one. All my insecurities about my abilities as a homeschool mom were put to rest as the kids thrived in school. Our older boys transitioned at semester break into grades eight and ten with the same positive experience. They loved their teachers and quickly made friends. My mama heart took a deep breath and released.

However, I hadn't realized how much homeschooling had sheltered us from the comparison game. I had never noticed how many of the kids' classmates were in sports. I would read their parents' posts on Facebook and wonder if I was being a completely delinquent parent by not spending my weekends at the hockey rink or at dance festivals. Our kids had always played the spring season of soccer, but suddenly I felt like we were limiting our kids' success by not doing more. I will tell you with all honesty that one of the hardest emotions I have ever experienced as a parent is feeling like I'm hindering my child's success at life, whether physical, spiritual, or emotional.

We moved to a neighbouring town during this time, and it didn't take long until I was in full-blown anxiety over my glaringly obvious lack as a mother. Our new hometown—which is fantastic, by the way—is a vibrant hockey community. The first question we got asked when meeting new people in town was "Which sports are your kids in?" or "Are your boys in hockey?" It was a culture shock to me, and I began to feel like less and less of a success in parenting. This was no one else's fault; I had incredible insecurities to begin with, and suddenly they were harshly illuminated by the spotlight I'd been unknowingly thrust into.

One night I went for a long walk, trying to process my anger and confusion and distress and grief. Anger at my parents for never encouraging me to do anything athletic. In fact, I wore only dresses, so many sports were simply not possible, not to mention we could never have afforded it even if it were a priority. Anger at my childhood church for teaching against organized sports. Confusion over how I could have gotten everything so wrong for so long. Distress at the state of my mind and the complete disaster I had so obviously turned out to be. And grief for the years I'd wasted not knowing I was doing it all wrong. Oh yes, I was a spicy stew of negativity on that walk. As I neared the hockey arena—ironically—I felt a sudden hush of peace fall on me, and the voice of God filled all my senses. It was nearly audible. "You've done well." The tears flowed freely as He reminded me of the years of soccer we did with the kids, watching them in rain, snow, wind, and sun, the years of karate that taught them discipline and respect, the years of classical piano lessons that taught them dedication and an appreciation for beauty.

But more than that, I was reminded of the decisions we'd made that brought our family together. We were becoming a unit that was tightly bonded. I didn't always love the word "family." I felt like some members of my own family had let me down in subtle ways since we'd made the choice to walk away from the church community that we'd grown up in. I felt like it was hard for me to want to hang out with my own biological family at holidays, and I deeply wanted different for the six of us. Sure, we sacrificed some things, things that most people deem important, like competitive sports and traditional schooling. But we had discovered what was important for us, and we acted on it, no matter how it looked or what people thought. The decisions we made were right for *our* family. Decisions that were made after much prayer and discussion.

I still have insecurities. They like to resurface, a lot. I thought parenting babies and toddlers was a challenge with all the Mommy Wars on breast- vs. bottle-feeding and cloth vs.

disposable diapers, but absolutely nothing prepared me for the internal pressure I felt with older kids and teenagers. I brought up my parenting insecurities with my therapist while I was still battling through the worst of it. I told her, "I really don't feel like I'm a good mom." Through expert questioning, she got me to admit what I thought a good mom did for her kids.

- A "good mom" was up early. (I like to sleep in.)
- A "good mom" always had hot meals on the table on time. (I'm usually trying to meet deadlines.)
- A "good mom" met them at the door with fresh cookies after school.
- A "good mom" was always available and not working.

Then she asked me if there was one more thing I could have received from my own parents, what would that be? It took me a moment, but only a moment. I often felt I couldn't be completely open and honest with my parents because I was scared it would come back in judgment on me. I didn't feel fully safe to open up about the things I struggled with and dreamed about as a teenage girl. As soon as I uttered the word "safe," all the floodgates opened. I looked at my therapist and replied, "Safe. A good mom is a safe place. I'm already a good mom."

I wish I could tell you exactly how I got to this place, where my teenage boys love to hang out with me in the kitchen, telling jokes and sharing about their evening out. But I'll be honest, I don't really know what I did to deserve these amazing young men. A lot of my parenting journey feels like stumbling and surprises, but if I had to make a guess, the biggest gifts we can give our kids are authenticity and humility. I need to be real with them and not pretend I'm flawless, and I need to be humble enough to apologize when I've missed the mark.

As a teenager, I vowed that even if I screwed up a million different ways, I wanted to acknowledge when I'd hurt my kids and give a genuine apology. This has simply never gone wrong for me. My kids are the most tender, forgiving, and compassionate people I will ever have the pleasure of knowing. I look back on nearly eighteen years of sticky hugs and emerging deep voices reassuring me that "It's okay, Mommy" or "I forgive you." The payoff is so worth any discomfort the apology can create.

If you feel like you're not measuring up in the parenting department, or that you're messing up your kids, I want you to know that:

- Your concern shows you care. In one of my counselling sessions where we focused on parenting, my therapist leaned in and said, "You need to hear this. If you are worried you're messing up your kids, it shows that you give a crap. You care. You are a good parent." I've witnessed parents who didn't care, who had no idea they were royally screwing up their kids. This comforted me so much, knowing that my lack of confidence that I was their best mom *simply showed that I was working toward being their best mom.*

- Apologizing is a superpower. I can't stress this enough. We all know we're screwing up sometimes, so to pretend otherwise is lying. When we as parents, humbly admit, "Hey, I was out of line, and I shouldn't have yelled at you," we give them a reason to trust us plus the permission to be honest themselves. Kids learn so much more from watching what we do than from what we tell them to do.

- Kids don't care about the stuff. We've always given our kids the option to receive physical gifts on their birthdays or invite their friends (or family) on an "experience" such as mini golf, escape room, trampoline park, arcade, etc. Once they reach a certain age, they always pick the experience. Ten years down the road they won't necessarily remember the gifts you gave them, but they will remember an extravagantly fun day spent with their friends or family. Your presence is worth so much more than presents.

"Unspoken expectations are premeditated resentments."

—Neil Strauss

On Faith.

The church I grew up in had a liturgical rhythm that was both comfortable and comforting. There was stability in the dress codes and meeting order. The familiar hymns were sung a cappella with beautiful harmonies. We all learned to sing from toddlerhood, and harmonizing was second nature. I liked the simple familiarity of knowing exactly what to expect from church.

Every winter, our church community held "revival meetings" for about two weeks— nightly church meetings with lots of teaching. This was considered a time to clean up and get yourself pure and ready for the annual communion service. For someone like me who placed a lot of value on how I was perceived by the people around me, it was often a time of stress and anxiety.

The visiting ministers who came to our community to teach these revival meetings expected to visit with each of us in our own homes to see how we were doing and to potentially give direction if needed. I was so concerned about impressing these visitors I'd scrub the house from top to bottom and spend hours cooking a meal that was good but simple as we usually had to rush off to the evening service. I dressed simply and made sure my hair was within the guidelines. I was a model Mennonite wife, and I knew I could make a good impression. I learned how to speak in a way that made me look good yet humble. I hated myself for the two people I was becoming.

I wanted to be good, to be well received by the church and by God. I didn't understand at that time that Jesus had already accepted me, which was all that mattered. When the time came for our members-only confession session, I dug deep for anything I could confess. Since I was already a rule-follower, often the worst I could come up with was that my clothing had gotten too fancy. I would confess what I could and found a certain level of peace around it.

I loved communion. It felt like a little moment in the year when everyone in the church was filled with love, peace, and acceptance. We were all on the same wavelength at that moment. It felt a little like I imagined Heaven would be. For a few weeks, things were just perfect. I could uphold whatever new resolutions I had committed to, but eventually, life happened, and my failures would stack up against me again. No matter how hard I tried, I couldn't maintain that level of perfectionism in my everyday raw, messy life.

I didn't fully understand that Jesus gave his life for me, individually, so that I could exit my loop of self-flagellation and despair, that I could live in hope and peace. The work had been done; I only needed to believe and accept. It would be a long time before this would become real to me.

In 2011, we made a hard decision that would change our lives forever. We had been through several hard years of wrestling with our beliefs within the church we'd grown up in. Our family was there; our friends were there; our whole life was there. But we couldn't deny the Voice that kept gently guiding us to search, to seek, to follow truth. One day in early 2011, after crying out to God for wisdom and guidance, I "felt" the voice of God almost audibly, filling my being. "You are not flourishing where you are."

The next Sunday we started attending a church an hour away, one that we'd watched online for over a year. It was a difficult decision that turned into a difficult year, but every Sunday the Holy Spirit washed over me, over us, in waves of grace. In that year, when we faced some shunning from some—but gratefully not all—of our family members and friends, I learned what it meant to have Jesus as a best friend. I learned that being alone in the world wasn't the worst thing; in fact, it showed me how deeply Jesus cared and understood. When he picked up the cross that spelled freedom for me, he was utterly and totally alone. Not even his Father stood with him in that moment.

Since then, in every circumstance that left me feeling alone or grief-stricken, I knew to lean into him. I knew that I could pray and converse with Jesus just as I would with a close friend. No fancy words, no pretending, just simple, raw honesty.

After a lifetime of worrying what people thought about me, I left the close-knit church of my childhood and embraced the freedom of finally learning to not take every cue from the people around me. It was dizzying for a while, not having tight boundaries to bump up against. But I learned to lean on the Holy Spirit a whole lot more. It took years to find my footing and feel grounded, but our new church family kept spreading Jesus's love and grace all over us, and it has always felt like Home when we're together. I still fall into the old habits of worrying about what people are thinking, but it's less often now. I know that we are all unique and what I choose may be a very different path than the person in the pew beside me or down the street from me. I spent too much time feeling resentful toward people and systems from my past, but I've learned this: Even though we may worship differently, we worship the same Jesus. We are not fighting against each other; we are fighting for the light, together.

If you're stuck in your faith journey, spending all your energy worrying that you're not enough, I encourage you to take a moment.

Step outside of church responsibilities for a second and take some time to just listen. Sit in the pew on Sunday morning and soak it in, let the worship wash over you. Learn to speak to Jesus with raw authenticity—he can handle it. Pour out *all* your frustrations and questions and doubts in prayer. None of it is too much for Jesus to take.

Next, get connected in a faith community.

Get involved in kids' ministry, join a small group of people with similar interests or in the same life stage as you, join the worship team, volunteer at a women's shelter or soup kitchen. Look for Jesus, not perfection, everywhere you go. "If you look for me wholeheartedly, you will find me" (Jeremiah 29:13 NLT).

Remember, your faith is in God, not humanity.

Humans are broken. Everyone has the potential to let you down, and when it happens, remember to separate the creation from the Creator. With a solid foundation and unshakable trust in Jesus, you cannot be crushed.

Keep it simple.

With our kids, we sit down once each week to connect with God as a family. We stick to a simple prayer template based on an Anne Lamott book: Help, Thanks, Wow. While we don't follow it perfectly, we aim to do three things:

1. Ask God for help either for ourselves or others.
2. Thank Him for what's good in our lives.
3. Express awe at who He is and what he's doing.

"Those who have a strong sense of love
and belonging
have the courage to be imperfect."

—Brené Brown

On Personalities.

Learning about my personality, specifically what my inner motivations are, has helped me immensely. I highly recommend digging into a personality assessment on some level to learn more about yourself and the people you live with. Not only will you understand yourself better but you will also be able to show up as a more fully authentic version of yourself in your family, your community, your business, and your church or school.

A simple book to start with is *Colorful Personalities* by George J. Boelcke (even better if you can find someone local who does a live presentation on this). It's an easy-to-understand five-minute quiz and very eye-opening.

If you want to go deeper, Myers-Briggs and the Enneagram are both great resources for understanding yourself and working with your strengths and through your weaknesses. My personal favourite is the Enneagram. Google can be your friend here, but I highly recommend digging into a book or podcast that explains it in lay terms to begin with. I appreciate how the Enneagram approaches from the perspective of weakness. I don't need more "rah-rah, you're doing a great job." I want to hear what motivates my actions and gather the tools for fixing what isn't working.

If you already understand the languages I'm speaking, you've probably guessed that I'm an Enneagram Nine with a One wing. My Nine core drives me to desire peace and being accepted by everyone, while my One wing drives me to crave control and perfectionism. All personality traits have both strengths and weaknesses.

When I'm not living in a place of balance and health, I'm controlling and avoidant. Alternatively, when I'm in a position of growth, I can use my Nine core to create peace and harmony, to mediate difficult situations, and to share the beauty I see in every moment. I can use my One wing to be organized and productive, manage my time well, strategize, set goals, and knock them out of the park. In my personal life, I research trips and plan events, and I make sure everyone has food to eat and knows what to bring to school the next day.

Because I'm so good at organizing and tying up the little details, I often feel like I'm indispensable. When I'm unhealthy, I start thinking that my family won't be able to function without me. This almost always leads to resentment, and it is simply not true. If I have to leave for a day or two, the world actually doesn't end. Will the kids end up at school with the same clothes or lunch I would have picked? No. Will the kids end up at school with clothes and lunches? Without a doubt, yes.

Any personality assessment can be misused, especially if you're using it as a way to excuse bad behaviour. But it can be invaluable in learning about yourself and the people in your life, to strengthen your relationships.

For example, my husband is (I think) an Enneagram 6. When the pandemic first hit in early spring of 2020, he would obsess about the news and do a ton of research and relay it all to me. All day. Every day. The heaviness of what the world was facing already weighed on me, and hearing this aggressive amount of info was too much for me. I finally asked him to stop sharing everything and just give me the CliffsNotes version if it was important.

Then I took a moment. And I researched the Enneagram 6. Turns out, all that "worst-case scenario" stuff they do? It's because they want to be prepared for all possibilities so they can protect their loved ones. My husband's "annoying" behaviour was him ultimately showing love to me. It changed my heart. I felt loved, protected, valued. Take the time to learn about the people you love. Find out what motivates them. It may just change everything for you.

I'm all emotion and heart and fickle feelings, while my husband is intellectual, factual, follow the data. We complement each other perfectly. I think there is something beautiful about figuring out how our personalities can mesh, work together, and create something stronger and more powerful than I could ever create on my own. Together, we are a force to be reckoned with.

Take some time to figure out your own personality first.

No pointing fingers or shaming, just educating yourself. Learn your weaknesses and embrace your strengths. Be open to learning hard things.

Then learn with your partner or family members.

Learn how your personalities work together and how they may clash at times. Knowledge is power. Becoming a "power couple" is 100% possible when you understand yourself and your partner. Become a better parent or employee or friend simply by gaining the understanding of how we function internally.

"Live authentically. Why would you continue to compromise something that's beautiful to create something that is fake?"

–Steve Maraboli

On What Defines Me.

I am the youngest of ten children. My middle name is Anne with an *e*. I am one of the rare people who actually does like kale.

These are things that are true about me, but are they who I am? What about when I try to rewrite the narrative on who I am?

I was heavily sheltered in my childhood home, and I don't fault my parents. They loved me deeply and protected me from a lot of hurt and evil, and for that I'm so grateful. What I was also sheltered from was adventure and freedom and discovering who I was apart from first my parents and then my husband. I went straight from my childhood home to my married adult home, and while hormones will carry anyone for a length of time, through marital relationships and mothering, there came a moment when I hit a breaking point.

It was in our third year of homeschooling and a year into my professional organizing business. I was beginning to burn out. As an introvert and a highly sensitive person, I found that parenting four kids 24/7 as well as being their sole educator were wearing me down. I didn't feel I was doing a very good job anymore, and I longed for a reset, a way to find my inspiration again.

Then an opportunity presented itself. It felt way "out there," and I wasn't sure we could afford it or make it work. But it started niggling in my mind: a writing retreat in the Cinque Terre region of Italy. I'd dreamed of being a writer my whole life. I'd dreamed of travelling to Italy for at least fifteen years. I loved everything I knew of the sun-soaked country, and it was a bucket-list item that I really didn't expect to fulfill. In my world, women didn't travel across the world by themselves. I didn't know why, but I needed to do this.

Then I did a thing that I don't necessarily recommend, but it was the only big decision I've ever made all on my own. I booked the three-day women's writing retreat, and then I told my husband. I think I needed him to know how deeply I wanted this. I remember sitting in the vehicle with him and saying, "I need you to park while I tell you something." We parked, and I explained what I'd done. "Can I buy the plane tickets for a week in Italy?" I asked him, expecting him to be shocked, grief-stricken, maybe flat-out refuse. What I didn't expect was his gracious, "It's your money too. If you need to do this, then do it." I'm not sure I'd ever loved my husband as much as I did right then.

For weeks I learned basic Italian on Duolingo. I became an expert on all things related to travel, Europe, and staying safe as a solo woman traveller. Despite being a chronic overpacker, I researched my way into a regular-sized campus backpack. I knew the Cinque Terre was home to steep, rocky terrain and cobblestone streets, so it simply wasn't practical to bring roller luggage. I knew exactly how many clothes I could get away with and what would be available in my room. I made sure my curling iron was compatible with the European standard 220-volt outlet so I wouldn't wreck it, plus I bought the type-C converter. There are moments being a perfectionist and information hog is a good thing!

Italy was everything I dreamed of. It was breathtakingly beautiful. My window overlooked the Ligurian Sea in the loveliest village of Riomaggiore. I loved having my window open, smelling the salty sea, and listening to the distant chatter of tourists and clatter of dishes in little seaside restaurants. I felt like I was in a dream that entire week. I met beautiful, talented, and inspiring women from all over North America and Europe at my three-day retreat. Once it was over, I spent a few days on my own, exploring and absorbing the culture. I hiked the cliffs high above the sea, from Monterosso to Vernazza, in the sweltering heat. I caught trains and interpreted signs, gorged myself on the fresh calamari and anchovies, and quenched my thirst on Aperol Spritz. I booked a cooking class with a private chef, and every moment I felt as if I was a character in a movie. Under his guidance and broken English, I pulverized the fresh basil into a delicious pesto and struggled to make the gnocchi as deftly as he instructed. I embraced the solo journey and felt so very, very much alive.

Will I do this trip again on my own? Probably not. I know I want to bring my husband along next time. But did I *need* to do that trip on my own? Absolutely. When I flew back into the Calgary airport at 1:00 on a Sunday afternoon and saw my family waiting, I burst into tears. Tucking her sweet little strawberry-blonde head into my neck, my six-year-old daughter said, "You look so happy, Mommy."

You see, I'd lost myself a little. I didn't know who I was aside from someone's daughter, someone's wife, someone's mom. I discovered that I need to get away sometimes, that I love adventure, and solo travel is probably my favourite thing in the whole world. I was *created* with this desire to explore the earth, to experience different cultures and foods and languages.

This trip also lit the first spark that I could potentially be a professional writer. The first night in Riomaggiore, running on close to zero hours of sleep over the previous twenty-four hours, I met my fellow female "retreaters" from countries around the world—France, Belgium, Italy, the US, and Canada. We bonded over bright lemon risotto, salty anchovies scooped fresh from the sea, and basil-laden pizzas. As we toasted each other with vibrant local wines, one of the women asked this question: "If you could do anything you wanted, but it couldn't be in your current industry, what would your career be?" Without hesitation, I surprised myself by saying, "A travel blogger!" I just knew that I wanted to be able to travel and write.

It's possible I won't ever be a travel writer, and that's okay.

But sometimes we have to take those terrifying and exhilarating steps outside our comfort zone to explore what could be... and it could end up changing our lives. If I hadn't taken the chance to do something wildly out of my comfort zone, I'm almost certain you wouldn't be holding this book in your hand today.

Writing. Travelling. That is what I enjoy, *but that's not what defines me.* Who I am is beloved, created, and equipped. Italy or Canada, writer or mom, I am fully whole as I am. Imperfect as I am.

I think it's also possible—and important!—to accept and celebrate who we are but also to not be content to stay there. I can cling to my need to be alone, to have a sparkling house, or just to be "comfortable" and use those as excuses to stay stuck.

I do prefer to be alone, but it can become a wall of defence to keep people out.

I do enjoy having a magazine-perfect house, but it's not always practical with four kids and can replace quality time together if I'm always scurrying around, tidying.

I do like my comfort zone, but what if there are pieces of myself I can grow and expand by stepping out once in a while?

I still get excited at the prospect of a night or two by myself in a hotel—that probably won't ever change. I was always independent, even as a young child. I still prefer working out by myself, going for long walks by myself, and shopping by myself. Maybe it's because I had nine siblings and never really had my own time or space. Or maybe it's because I got married young and had four children. Or maybe, maybe I was created to be still and deep and creative and emotional. It may take me a lifetime to figure out fully what my Creator has in mind for me and to embrace the journey.

Celebrate who you are.

Embrace the parts that make you who you are. There's no shame in admitting that you enjoy your own company or prefer a quiet night in with a good book to a night of partying. You may feel you are too much of something—too indoorsy, too quiet, too loud, too colourful—and not fit the mold you think you need to fit into. But you were created *just exactly the way you are.* You fill a spot that no one else can, and you add just the right amount of colour and sound to your corner of the world.

Acknowledge that there is always room for improvement.

Just because I want to be alone and constantly avoid the outside world doesn't mean it's the best thing for me or the people I love. I'm a fan of lifelong learning and growing. I support the concept that I can adjust my beliefs when I come upon new information. I can love my body as it is and still want to exercise and work on my fitness and strength. I can accept that I'm a good mom but still work at being a better mom. There is always opportunity for growth and learning.

"You are imperfect, permanently and inevitably flawed. And you are beautiful."

—Amy Bloom

On Body Image.

One of the most impactful places perfectionism has shown up in my life is in my health and fitness journey. With an all-or-nothing mindset, I've felt that I couldn't get healthy without doing a hard-core keto diet or having professionally created workout plans. I have found the opposite to be true. My schedule and habits are anything but perfect. I don't usually get up before 7:00, I work out weirdly in the middle of the afternoon, using only machines I like. I no longer weigh and measure daily as if my life depends on it. I have no idea if I'm losing weight and honestly don't care too much. And yet... Working out daily is bringing me SUCH JOY. You have to understand, I have always *hated* working out. This is so completely unlike me and so incredibly freeing. Nothing compares to the hit of endorphins from a good hour of intentional movement. It may not be perfect, it's not always pretty, but dang, it feels good. It was definitely not always this way.

I've been a professional dieter for many, many years. I never thought of myself as "fat" until I'd been on the birth control pill and gained thirty pounds within the first few years of marriage. Add in four babies over the next nine years, a total weight gain of sixty-plus pounds, and I started to feel like my body was flawed and needed to be "fixed." Cue a vicious cycle of various diets, usually involving a zero-carb element. I quickly assigned morality to food—low in sugar was "good," high in carbs was "bad." I avoided carrots, peas, onions, and definitely fruit because they were too high in sugar. I joined Facebook groups where everyone was just like me—all or nothing. If you were "lazy keto" instead of fully committed keto, you got called out. We all thought we were supporting each other. A LOT of weight was lost... I lost and gained back the same forty pounds repeatedly.

When I was 29, I discovered I loved running. I found the solitude refreshing and the discipline rewarding. I signed up for my first 10k race in 2011. It was a big year for me; we had just made a huge life change by leaving the only church and social group we'd ever known, I was turning 30 in September, and we decided to get pregnant for the fourth and last time. I trained faithfully all summer, and the race happened to be just days before my 30th birthday. I was emotional and devastated that entire race because I'd gotten my period that morning, and this was the first time in our entire marriage that I hadn't gotten pregnant exactly when planned. I know, I was a rookie to this whole waiting game, but I was a wreck. I remember running that entire 10 kilometres with a heavy heart, tears often streaming down my face. I found a running buddy who stuck with me the whole way and supported me. I finished my first-ever 10k race in 1:09, and I have never been prouder of anything! The "runner's high" lasted for about two days.

Running was so good. But in the back of my mind, I was always doing it to fix my broken self. To repair the version of me that was too big for society. With this mindset, there was nothing I could do that would ever be "enough." And so I dropped running and working out of any kind. I continued a vicious cycle of dieting that would last a couple of weeks, quit when it felt hopeless, then I'd pick myself up again and pretend I didn't care. Eventually, I got to the place where I really did accept my body how it was... when I wasn't wearing anything. But when I tried to put clothes on, I always felt off. Nothing fit quite right, so I started buying excessive amounts of clothing in a desperate attempt to make myself feel like I belonged.

Every month when the credit card statement came, I winced

and hoped my husband wouldn't see all the charges. I bought luxuriously soft sweaters and satin blouses, cute boots and jeans, and dresses. I got a rush every time the doorbell rang with another online order but felt quickly deflated after trying everything on and feeling not-quite-right again. I was still stuck in this body that "didn't work." I would shop and spend more money to try to make myself into who I thought I should look like.

At the time, I was in an entrepreneur group with six women who supported each other in intense personal growth. I worked up the nerve one day to bring up my shopping problem. I was asked the question, "Why are you looking for your identity in your clothing?" It brought me up short. Why, indeed? I am a believer in a Creator who makes no mistakes. I know that I was painstakingly "knit in my mother's womb" (Psalm 139:13–14 NIV) and that I'm on this earth because the God of the universe looked at the planet and felt that it needed someone like me. So why, I asked myself, am I working so hard and spending so much time and money to force myself into something I'm not? I had to take a hard look at who I really believed I was. I looked at my C-section scars and stretch marks, my worry lines and cellulite, my extra bits of padding and saggy parts that don't fit most clothing lines... If God was happy, if he "delighted" in me (Zephaniah 3:17 NIV), then who was I trying to impress?

As I started to see my body as fully created and fully loved, I began to love it a little more myself. I began to work out because it felt good. I'd go to spin class and look down at my legs flying on those pedals and think, "Look how strong my legs are and how hard they can work. Thank you, legs, for supporting me wherever I go." Was the workout still really hard, and did it take a Herculean effort to get my butt in that bike seat at 6:20 a.m.? Yes. But I was no longer doing it to "fix" myself. I did it out of pure delight in the fact that my body *could*.

In 2019, we moved to a town with an actual gym—the type of gym you can go to 24/7 with the swipe of a keycard. I learned that within those walls, I could try things. I could lift weights, something I'd always been intimidated by. I found a YouTube video that explained the foundation for a good workout routine and built my own around that. I found that back squats and lat pull-downs are my favourites. I also learned that I didn't have to create a perfectly designed plan every time I hit the gym. All movement is good movement. Some days when grief and emotions and hormones raged within, I just hit the stationary bike for an hour. At first, I stressed about looking like a worn-out, middle-aged woman just sitting lazily on a bike, but I eventually learned to not worry about that either. No one knows the struggle that goes on in the minds of the people around us. I learned to give grace to others at the gym too.

I discovered I loved going for walks. All my life I thought activity had to be, you know, Activity with a capital A. I found incredible joy in going for long walks around town. I had no distractions and could focus on the beauty of the sunrise, the crispness in the air, the activity of a small town waking up. I recently learned the term "awe walk" and realized that's why I loved it so much. An "awe walk" is when you go for a walk and intentionally focus your attention on the beauty around you instead of whatever's going on inside you. My creativity comes alive when I'm walking, and this book would absolutely not have happened without all those five-to-ten-kilometre jaunts and voice recording software.

One night a few years ago, my husband and I went to an event in the city that commanded an elevated dress code. I had fun picking out a dress that was colourful and fun yet comfortable. We enjoyed the beverages and food as we mingled and networked, connecting with old friends and making new ones. The speaker, Molly Bloom, told her riveting story, the evening was memorable, and I felt fully alive. As we headed out the door, an acquaintance stopped me and said, "Congratulations!" I looked at her, utterly confused, until I realized she had made an assumption that I was pregnant. A few awkward moments ensued, during which she tried to apologize and appropriate replies simply failed me. We took our coats and continued out the door. I wouldn't say I was hurt; I was more stunned. I'd never had this happen before!

The next day, a friend I hadn't seen in a while popped by. She took one look at me and said, "You look so great! Did you know you've inspired me to start back up on Weight Watchers? I've seen how hard you've worked and how it's paid off."

You know what? You'll never be enough if you listen to the external opinions about your body. In the space of twelve hours, I'd been labelled as "pregnant" and then "weight-loss inspiration." I'm grateful for these two experiences as they taught me not to look outward for my identity. Graciously, I could move forward, not faulting either woman for their opinion of me but also not putting too much into what they said. I could hop off the roller coaster of others' approval and know that I was still enough just as I was.

You are created and whole just as you are.

The day you were born, the angels sang because you were perfect and whole and beautiful. Those truths haven't changed. The number on the scale or measuring tape, the shape and colour of your eyes, the texture of your hair, the melanin or lack thereof are all created in an amount that are perfectly, beautifully you. There will always be voices saying you need more of this and less of that. Ignore them. Practice looking in the mirror and saying, "I'm created, I'm whole, I'm beautiful, I'm loved."

You are needed.

Your voice, your smile, your story, and your song are all desperately needed in a broken, aching world. Use the voice that some say is too loud to bring justice and peace to the oppressed. Use the song that quavers a little to bring hope and light to the hurting. Use your colour and joy and vibrance—the traits that have always felt like "too much"—to bring life to the walking, breathing dead. Mark Twain is quoted as saying: "The two most important days in your life are the day you are born and the day you find out why." Maybe the parts you are most self-conscious about, the parts that feel so imperfect and inadequate, are exactly the parts that are needed by the people you meet every day.

You have a purpose.

Hold your head up a little higher, allow that spring in your step. You're alive. You have a world to explore and people to love. You have a body that houses a beating heart and simply won't stop. Make this the day that you find out why and live it every day of your life.

"Life is messy and gloriously imperfect, and some signs of wear and tear indicate a well-loved, well-used home."

—Deborah Needleman

On Home and Hospitality.

I love having people over. I will qualify that by saying I do like some warning. As an introvert and internal processor, I find it hard to switch gears quickly when it involves being with other people unexpectedly. But I do love sharing my home with people I love and new people I'm just getting to know. I love offering up my home as a safe and comfortable place to connect and support each other. I love having deep, enriching conversations and laughing till our bellies hurt. I love holding hands and praying as the tears flow. I love living, fully alive, and inviting others to join in.

One of the most beautiful things about the culture I grew up in is the high priority placed on hospitality. We were always inviting people over and making food to feed anywhere from ten to thirty people. We grew most of our own food and learned how to make simple dishes from a pretty young age. At 13, I was baking dinner buns and apple pies from scratch. I was also sewing all my own clothes. At 13, I had sewing, cooking, baking, gardening, and canning figured out. By the time I got married at 18, I was over it and wasn't sure I ever wanted to see a garden again. I went through a very long rebellion where I didn't grow or sew anything.

One day I came to the realization that it really was okay. It was okay whether I was or wasn't into all the domesticities of my Mennonite upbringing. It was okay if I wanted to have a huge garden or none at all. It was okay if I made everything from scratch or bought our clothes and baked goods. It was okay as long as my motivation wasn't from perfectionism and pressure. It was okay as long as it was authentic to me. I realized that I was rather "indoorsy," and I started to embrace it. I preferred organizing, redecorating, and decluttering to puttering in a garden for hours. I realized I wanted a career despite my culture having taught me that moms stayed home.

We moved in 2019, just forty-five kilometres to the west. The house we'd lived in for the past 11 years was one we'd planned and designed ourselves. It wasn't our dream home, and we'd always known we'd upgrade one day. That day came a little quicker than we'd planned for, but we were able to purchase a new build, a spec house, in a neighbouring town. I loved the idea of once again living in a home that no one had lived in before us. I know some people love the history and character of old homes, but I love the blank canvas of a new home. And what a lovely blank canvas this was! The house was smaller than we were used to but so much brighter and more modern. I loved it. I loved that I finally had a fireplace, which was a lifelong dream of mine. I loved my pure white cabinets, white quartz countertops, and white subway tile.

But a curious thing happened when we had guests over. I found myself pointing out the imperfections and the things I didn't like.

"I really wish this laundry room was wider."

"I hate these light fixtures. They're so generic!"

And on and on, ad nauseum. Why was I dissing my lovely home? Of course, there were imperfections and things we would have planned differently if we'd contracted the house ourselves. But did that make it a bad home for us? Where was my gratitude?

I started making a conscious effort to focus on our guests when we were entertaining and not on my home. No apologies, no complaining, no discontentment. Just relaxed and meaning-ful conversation.

When I focus my energy outward, gratitude grows within. I want a messy life full of good food and laughter with mismatched friends. We don't have to all look the same, think the same, or talk the same. In fact, I want to be able to learn from every person who crosses my threshold. All I hope to offer is peace, love, acceptance, and a lot of laughter.

I grew up reading The Baby-Sitters Club as a kid and wishing I had that close group of friends that walked in and out of each other's houses all the time. We always lived rural, and I thought how amazing it would be to just be able to bike or walk to each others' houses. I've become a small-town girl over the past twelve years and wouldn't trade it for anything. I love having neighbours I can visit with as we're watering flowers, neighbours who text when we leave our garage door open, neighbours who have become friends. As I grow older, my circle grows a bit smaller but oh so much richer and deeper.

On my 39th birthday, six months into the pandemic, we went to church as usual, and my husband surprised me on our way home by turning into my beloved local Italian restaurant. We stuffed ourselves with a decadent meal of bruschetta, calamari, and fresh pasta before heading home. As I walked into the house, I saw through to the backyard, which was filled with some of my dearest friends.

My heart burst into a kaleidoscope of shock, joy, and grief. It had been a hard six months of restrictions and anxiety and loss, and somehow seeing my backyard full of beautiful souls who chose to spend their Sunday celebrating me was almost more than I could take. In all the best possible ways.

When I get caught up in discontent and complaining, all I need to do is refocus on what's really important.

If anything good came out of 2020, it's this: What really matters is raw, unfiltered, face-to-face connection with the people we love. Your house doesn't matter. Your people will love you no matter where you lay your head at night. Your thread count and silverware don't make one bit of difference to the people who really matter. If external voices have more clout in your life than the people you know and love intimately, consider turning off social media or TV for a while. Take a break from disappearing into a novel or Netflix and be intentional about human connection.

When you lose someone, whether due to death or diverging values, or you need to adjust and refocus your dreams due to a pandemic, the economy, or your health, everything comes into focus.

"Having it all" is not only impossible, but it's not even desirable. The greatest beauty in life often comes from wildly chaotic beginnings that we wouldn't choose for ourselves, from authentic gatherings of mismatched friends who will laugh, cry, and pray with you, allow you in, and love you for who you are. There's just simply no room for "perfect" in a rich and beautiful life.

When you're tempted to complain about the house you live in, take out a stack of sticky notes and write things you're grateful for in your home.

It can be as basic as "indoor plumbing" or "hot showers." Stick these notes around your home where you can't miss them. Change them up as needed.

When you can't see beyond the flaws and imperfections of your home, step outside and spend some time helping someone who has less.

Remember, when you focus your energy outward, gratitude grows within.

"...it is love, imperfect and unordered, that keeps them apart, even as it holds them somehow together..."

—Judith Guest

On the Hardness of Holidays.

The holiday season can be an intense and sometimes difficult time. Many of us have a magnified feeling of pressure, often internally, to create a "magical" or "perfect" holiday for our families.

But let's be honest, every family has dysfunction. There are varying political opinions, religious opinions, and now the added pandemic opinions. There are polarizing views at nearly every table, and it simply brings its own layer of stress. None of us has a perfect family. None of us share all the same views as other members of our family. We differ on religion, politics, stances on social issues, parenting and lifestyle choices... the list goes on.

In the past few years, I've grown to dread Christmas. I don't want to be a Grinch, but I've started feeling Grinch-y. Sometimes I just want to fly away to a beach in the Caribbean until it's all over. Twenty years ago, John Grisham published a book titled *Skipping Christmas*, which later birthed the movie *Christmas with the Kranks*. From the first time I read that book, I dreamed of how we could pull off skipping Christmas ourselves.

Recently we visited my aging parents. My dad's time on earth is limited, and we make the six-hour drive whenever we can. In our last visit, my mom mentioned that when we're young and busy with our families, it's all such a blur and we don't realize how the older ones need us and crave the time together. They appreciate the noise and chaos that comes with a family. They have lived a full life and are deeply grateful for the quality time they can spend with people they love. It took me by surprise. I didn't realize how much I'd made the holidays about me and my comfort.

I had focused on myself and my discomfort while visiting family.

I had focused on the sacrifices I'd made to drive long distances in holiday traffic.

I had focused on the inconvenience of facing shopping mall crowds to buy for someone I love whose love language is gifts.

It's not about me.

Not one part of Christmas has ever been about me. From its lowly beginnings in a stable, the story of Christmas has always been about sacrifice, service, inconvenience, love, and self-lessness.

I still don't love big, commercialized holidays. I'd rather pick our own way of celebrating life in random ways. Midweek parties for no reason with people that mean everything to us. Giving gifts if/as we want to, in January or July or October. Avoiding the crowds and saving some sanity.

But I also have kids, and my daughter especially loves holidays. I want her to experience that too. We keep it pretty simple around here. We do a simple tree, a few simple gifts. We eat good food, play a few games, go sledding. This kind of holiday... I like it. It brings me closer to the manger. Closer to the birth of Christ in the most humble of delivery rooms. Closer to love, simplicity, sacrifice, peace, and joy.

I just want more of this and less of all the rest.

If you're a people pleaser like me, and the holidays just feel like an overwhelming series of events where you feel pulled in multiple directions, remember this:

- Show up authentically. I could be me in the kindest, most gracious way that I know how, and some people will still not like it. That's okay. I'll keep being myself, keep learning how I can show up well, and keep growing.

- Spread grace and kindness like a five-year-old spreads peanut butter. The holidays bring up a lot of emotions in many different people. A lot of people have no idea how to deal with those big feelings. Handle the holiday people with extra care. Some are facing the season for the first time without a parent, a child, or a close friend. Some are facing the people who've hurt them in the past. Some of "those people" might be you. Give yourself grace and kindness too.

Remember, people who need the most love often ask for it in the most unlovable ways.

"But above all, in order to be, never try to seem."

—Albert Camus

On Starting Over.

As a child showing off my white shoes, I wanted everyone to see them in their pristine state, with that faint new-rubber smell, but I knew they wouldn't stay that way. I still find myself wanting to show others when I'm bright and shiny and then disappear when my soul feels dusty and stained.

In my adulthood, I noticed this theme when stuff got real. Even as an introvert, I loved meeting new people and hearing their stories. We'd meet for coffee a few times and share our lives a little, but when it came to hard emotions and tough conversation, I'd disappear. I always thought I was in touch with my emotions. I cried easily, I empathized with people, I cared. But when it came to me being vulnerable—real vulnerability, not the curated kind—I was out. Those days when it felt like too much work to wash my hair, when my marriage felt like a hot mess, or I wondered why I'd thought it was a good idea to have any children at all, never mind four of them, were lonely days. Those were not the days I asked to meet someone for coffee.

My sweet, selfless friend Pauline got it. She'd show up at my door with lattes on the hardest days, and she looked right past the greasy hair and bloodshot eyes to the real me. She made me feel seen. It didn't matter how messy my life felt. She would start folding laundry and visit with me as if I was the most interesting person on the planet, and believe me, those days I really wasn't.

She had such a gift.

When we moved to a new community, I breathed a sigh of relief. This would be my clean slate. I would become my best self in every way. I purged our belongings to a level of minimalism that would make Marie Kondo proud. I bought new bedding for all the beds. I made sure our dishes and towels all matched and were on point for my décor style. But more than that, I decided it was time for a do-over of my personality. I would be less introverted and less of a hot mess. I would be the fun mom, the fit mom, the friendly mom, the put-together mom. We would be the fun family, the fit family, the friendly family, the put-together family. Oh, the fallacy!

For a while, it worked. We moved into a newly built home that was all bright and white and grey, with modern and clean lines. My soul felt bright and shiny too. It felt like a vacation for the first few months; we'd walk around the neighbourhood, and no one knew us. I loved the anonymity. I loved that I could be whoever I wanted to be. It was still a small town, but a 4,500-person small town, not an 800-person small town anymore. I no longer knew 80% of my community, nor was I known. No one knew the family traits and histories, no one cared where I came from. All they knew was the here and now. And oh, I could work with the here and now. The here and now was bright and shiny.

But that's not real life.

I'd love to tell you the story of me growing past this and embracing the real and raw. I'd love to share how I've gotten better at the hard conversations and embracing the hard people that God put in my life... but I don't think we ever fully get there. All I can say is I'm a work in progress, and Jesus's grace is so big.

It turns out you bring all those ugly bits with you when you move. It turns out when you move to a bright and shiny future, sometimes pandemics hit and dreams die, and so does your best friend. And you, a well-brought-up girl who was taught to be strong and work hard, to pull up your big-girl panties and push through? Well, you get shingles, anxiety attacks, and a depression diagnosis over the course of eighteen months. Your world may look perfect on the outside, but internally, it's in a state of emergency.

And so I'm learning to let go.

I'm learning that in "fight or flight," fight can sometimes mean irritability. I'm learning to work on regulating my emotions when I feel I'm plummeting out of control.

When I get stuck, I pray. I take a moment. I access the great mercies that "begin afresh each morning" (Lamentations 3:23 NLT).

I go for a walk without my earbuds. I keep the music and podcasts turned off. I take notice of the things I can hear, the things I can see, the things I can smell. I focus on my breathing. I think of three things I'm grateful for right now. No over-thinking.

I make the choice to not micromanage every move my kids make or criticize every time my husband does a household chore differently than I do. I try to rein in the irritability when someone pops in unexpectedly and the house is a disaster. I learn to let Jesus take the reins when it feels impossible to me.

We still have a lot of bumps, but we are learning to live with great intention.

I love what the ampersand (&) represents. I can be a hot mess AND yet worthy, impatient AND loving, uneducated AND also successful. Such a small word that holds so much hope. Leaning on Jesus makes the "and" possible in my life. The burden of holding everything together perfectly is simply too much for any human. That's what grace is for.

Find something that works for you in becoming more connected and authentic.

Here are a few things we've found to revolutionize our relationships.

- We go to church as a family. Spending that hour on the pew together every week cements our faith in something so much more powerful than just us, and it bonds us as a family.

- We spend weeknight dinners together around one table. One of my dearest memories of my childhood is lingering long around the dinner table. Having that time to connect with each other at the end of each day is vital to us now.
- We're real and raw together. The kids get to see how we maneuver challenges as adults. They see that we can do it imperfectly *and* well, with grief *and* hope, with anger *and* joy. The ever-present *and*.

"Material goods rarely alter our levels of happiness, unlike emotional experience. Having can never replace being."

—Ilsa Crawford

On Living in the "Everyday."

In my childhood home, and most of the homes I have spent time in, there were two sets of dishes, "everyday dishes" and "Sunday dishes." We pulled out all the stops for guests. The house was cleaned thoroughly on Saturdays since Sunday was the day we were most likely to invite someone over without planning ahead. The house was clean, the guest towels were hung, the good dishes brought out. I kept this tradition up well into our marriage.

Then, when I started to simplify our home a few years ago, I remember asking myself why we needed so many dishes. Why couldn't we use nice dishes and fluffy towels and have a tidy home when it was just us? I sold the everyday dishes and kept the nicer ones. I decluttered the silverware and kept just one set that was quality and would stand up to daily use. We turned guest towels into "towels." For several years now, we've used the nice stuff. Just for us. Just because. We never know what tomorrow holds, and maybe this is extra clear to me after losing someone close to me. We don't know if we have tomorrow or even tonight. Use the good silverware and towels, say "I love you" for no reason, eat good food, laugh, cry, apologize, breathe. Be vulnerable and authentic, and live fully, deeply now.

Now, we wear good clothes at home. Some days, I dress up and wear makeup even when I don't have a Zoom call. I put on red lipstick some days even if I don't leave my house. Are there some days I wear sweatpants and yesterday's mascara? Absolutely. And I have grace for those days too... sometimes we need to pull back. But if I feel like wearing a blouse and lipstick, I'm not going to wait for guests. All I have is here and now.

Taking care of my personal appearance on the daily when working from home has helped me in a number of ways.

- I'm more productive when I feel clean and put together. Trudging through the workday with greasy hair and bleach-stained sweats does not add up to a good productive day for me. How I start my day and what I choose to wear makes such a difference!
- I'm ready to go at a moment's notice if something does come up. If my husband wants to take me out for lunch or a friend texts that she wants to meet for coffee, I don't hesitate because my self-care is on point for the day.
- I have more compassion for the people I live with if I feel good about myself. When I feel grungy and unkempt, I'm not treating myself well and likely won't treat others well either.

Get into the habit of asking yourself, "Does this support the life I'm trying to cultivate?"

"Perfectionism is just fear in a more palatable package."

—unknown

On Fear.

I don't like the word "fear." I always want to get defensive and say, "But I don't feel like I'm afraid!" The thing is, fear doesn't always feel like fear. It can feel like anger, queasiness, addictive habits, insomnia, and—a biggie for me—imposter syndrome.

One winter when I was about 10, my friends invited me over after school to do some sledding. They had a little garage that they loved to climb up and sled off into deep snow drifts. This was northern Alberta, and snow was not in short supply. It was completely safe, and so I climbed up onto the shed roof and simply... froze. I wanted to slide down; it looked like a ton of fun as I watched them go, over and over again. I was stuck in my fears for an hour or more as my friends played. Finally, it was time for me to go home for supper and the only way down was to slide down. I had to do it. I let go. It was exhilarating! What a rush! I couldn't wait to go again... but I had to leave. I remember the sadness and disappointment I had in myself for not being able to let go of that fear earlier.

For a perfectionist, fear is often not of the thing we're facing but rather losing our illusion of control. I often say I'd love to go skydiving—and I really do hope to one day—because although I am terrified of heights and have control freak tendencies, I am oddly more than okay when I know I'm *not in control*. When I have the illusion of control, I feel overwhelmed with fear and anxiety. But when I can release that illusion and realize I really don't control a lot in this world beyond my own thoughts and reactions, there is peace. I believe that there is Someone so much more powerful than I am, who has the whole world and every intimate detail of my life in his hand. When I can grasp this Truth and surrender my worry and fear to Him, life simply works a lot better. I become a calm, strong woman who knows who she is and who's got her back.

"This is my command—be strong and courageous! Do not be afraid or discouraged. For the Lord your God is with you wherever you go" (Joshua 1:9 NLT).

My son just got his driver's license and started driving off to school every morning (how dare he!). While I knew this was coming and even anticipated it—especially the help with driving the kids to their activities and picking up groceries—I still feel a twinge of fear when he pulls out of the driveway. I know he's a good driver; I just feel like I'm losing control a little, and it terrifies me. Gone are the days I could keep them all within arm's reach and protect them from the various dangers that simply being alive presents them! Every time I watch him drive off, I take a deep breath. I remember that I was once 17, too, with a brand-new license. I was careless and reckless and did some stupid things, as all teenagers do. I can no more prevent my son from doing teenager-y things than my parents could with me.

In situations like this, I remind myself what my end goal is. What do I want for my son? I want him to be a generous and productive member of society. I want him to be adventurous and take a few risks. I want him to experience freedom. All of these things are made more possible with him driving. It's so easy to get stuck in our fear in the moment, but if we can take a step back and look at the bigger picture, everything comes into focus.

A few years ago, I signed up for a Tough Mudder race near me. I trained for months and was comfortably running a 10k by the time the day arrived. Nothing could have prepared me for the reality of an obstacle course—in the mud—on a September day that could have been lovely but chose to be 7°C (45°F) and raining. It was brutally cold, especially after the first obstacle that involved fully submerging in an ice-water tank. The race took four hours and every bit of grit that I could muster. The challenge was far more than physical, but the sense of community and camaraderie was so encouraging. At the start of the race, an energetic young man with a bullhorn gave us a pep talk to pump us up. I'll never forget him quoting Eleanor Roosevelt. "Do one thing every day that scares you."

I'm also terrified of deep water. It's a fact anyone who's been with me near a lake can attest to. I'm capable of swimming. I know this because I've taken *multiple* sets of adult swimming lessons. I know in theory that I can keep myself afloat, but just the thought of being in water and unable to touch the bottom gives me a jolt of adrenaline. Even as I type this, my heart skips a beat. Do I actually fear the water? No. I fear not being in control. I fear not being able to reach down and ground myself at any point rather than just going with the flow.

Big picture? I want to have fun with my kids. I don't want to continue missing out on the simple joys that life has to offer. One day, I want to leap into the deep end of a pool. I will continue to work on this goal through counselling, swimming lessons, and simply getting myself to where I can feel the fear and do it anyway. And when that happens, it will be the best gift I give myself. I'm such a work in progress. I don't have this all figured out, and it's okay if you don't either.

Even in the craziness of the past two years in our fear- and anger-driven world, it's possible to live in peace with hope for the future. I know this because I have complete peace over what happens next. While I hear the conflicting voices, the impassioned protests, and the vitriol that gets spewed on social media on a daily basis, I know who ultimately has control. He's the One who created it all. He knows our hearts and our vile capabilities. He knows every bit of truth about diseases, vaccines, and governments. He sees families and communities ripping each other apart over the divisive topic of the day. None of this is new or shocking to him. He knows how it ends. And because I trust Him, I do too. I don't fear tomorrow, whether it comes or doesn't, whether I die or not.

I've put my faith in Jesus Christ and trust that he's in control.
This has been the most empowering move I've made in my life. I've been told it's a crutch. I respect that if you've never experienced the perfect peace He gives, it's impossible to understand. But when my world starts shaking, I feel the most confident. Because I can't even pretend to hold the reins anymore. I let go, and I'm finally free from fear. Free to fully live.

I read Philippians 4:6-9 and tattoo these words on my heart:
> *Don't worry about anything; instead, pray about everything. Tell God what you need, and thank him for all he has done. Then you will experience God's peace, which exceeds anything we can understand. His peace will guard your hearts and minds as you live in Christ Jesus.*

> *And now, dear brothers and sisters, one final thing. Fix your thoughts on what is true, and honorable, and right, and pure, and lovely, and admirable. Think about things that are excellent and worthy of praise. Keep putting into practice all you learned and received from me—everything you heard from me and saw me doing. Then the God of peace will be with you.*

"We see Your strength and even though we're shaking, we know we are safe."

—Nicole Williams

On Vulnerability.

Emotions are messy and hard. I was taught from a young age to be stoic. Being the youngest of ten kids, I'm sure I cried more than my fair share. I remember being told to stop crying many times, and now as a mom who's very sensitive to noise, I understand this. But it taught me that crying isn't safe, that emotions are a burden to others. This is effective in silencing me because I hate being a burden.

As I near middle age and hard things happen with greater frequency, I find myself becoming avoidant. I bury myself in my work because it's safe and can't hurt me. I narcotize by disappearing into books or movies or mindless scrolling. I have become a crazy plant lady, filling my home and yard with every type of foliage and bloom. Name anything that lacks emotion or interaction and I'm there, fully invested.

Sometimes, I'm just tired of my mess. I'm ashamed of my mess. I feel like I should have it a little more together by now. Don't all women have it figured out by age 40? The answer is no, by the way, and the more I talk to women my age, the more I realize that none of us feel like we've got this 100% of the time. I think it's so important we share with vulnerability to let others know they're not alone and then support each other without judgment.

Here's what I've learned: Your mess doesn't ever go away.

Your mess is how people connect with you. In nearly fifteen years of sporadic blogging and Facebook-posting, my highest engagement and most comments *always* happen on posts that caused me to sweat a little before I hit "publish." Anxiety, depression, loneliness, feeling like a bad mom, feeling like I'm failing at life in general—these are all posts that had readers filling my DMs. I was told so many times that I was brave, that they wished they were courageous enough to be open about their struggle.

I don't feel particularly brave most of the time, but I do feel passionate about making people feel less alone. When all we see is a curated social media feed, it's so easy to feel "less than" our "competition." But it's not about competition, it's about human connection. It is vitally important that we connect with other humans in vulnerability and authenticity.

I don't think bravery and vulnerability are optional anymore. Social media isn't going away. The constant comparison will always be out there, but we can choose to opt out.

We can choose to change the narrative, send out the "real" over "highlight" reels, the joy of missing out over the fear of missing out, and self-acceptance over self-hate.

You can talk about anxiety or stretch marks on social media and not die. You may even make a few new friends, real friends. You can choose who you engage with, who you follow, or even if you want to walk away from all of it.

It's your decision.

You get to decide whether you present yourself to the world real and raw or masked and filtered. You decide whether you want deep and lasting relationships or ones that are filled with distrust and competition. If you find your relationships are shallow and unfulfilling, it might be time to take a look at how you're showing up. What are you choosing to bring to the relationship?

"No matter what your age or your life path, whether making art is your career or your hobby or your dream, it is not too late or too egotistical or too selfish or too silly to work on your creativity."

—Julia Cameron

On Being an Artist.

I have always rejected the idea that I was an artist. I felt that to embrace that title, I needed to work with a medium like paint or clay or that I needed to play an instrument or sing in a band. I spent such a large part of my life not creating because writing was just a silly hobby, and who would want to read what I wrote anyway?

I wrote compositions in school for English class and loved it. I wrote poetry to assuage my teenage angst, and I kept a journal through the tumultuous year of "not dating" my now-husband. But I didn't continue writing. Not for several years until after I was a mom and started a "mommy blog" in 2007 titled "Between Loads of Laundry." It was just for fun—never a career—but it lit me up and filled my soul. I wrote about the surprises of parenting babies and toddlers. I invited my readers to celebrate milestones with me and commiserate on teething and potty-training challenges. I shared products that made my life easier and recipes that even the pickiest of kids would eat.

I even had a brief stint—between babies—of blog design work for other mommy bloggers. I immensely enjoyed creating beautiful spaces for these women to showcase their own writing and online shops. Although I had no formal graphic design training, I loved the work of making beautiful things and tweaking the Blogger coding to match each client's branding and style.

But I still wasn't an "artist." Nor did I call myself a writer. Those labels were terrifying, and I felt desperately unworthy. Why was I so afraid to claim my talents and embrace the gifts I was given?

I didn't understand that making delicious and colourful food was art, that my home was my canvas, and that the furniture and décor I loved to play with were my mediums. I couldn't see that planting flower gardens for no purpose other than adding beauty was the definition of artistry.

And I definitely didn't recognize my pen as my most powerful and effective tool in reaching people and helping others see another side to a story or to feel less alone.

I thought that to be an artist I had to be drawing or painting or singing, but I now believe all of us have a bit of art inside of us. All of us have a piece of us that is creative. We were created by an Artist, a Creator, and we were made in His image, so why would we not be creators too?

So when you are moved by a beautiful sunset and you lift your phone to take a picture, you're engaging in an act of art in collaboration with the Creator. When you plant flowers and paint your house or your nails or your hair, you're creating pockets of beauty that make this world a brighter and better place.

Remember, whether you create art in your garden, your kitchen, or your place of work, and whether your instrument is a pen, a spatula, or a paintbrush, you are an artist.

So dig in to what lights you up and brings beauty to the world in some small way.

"When I see you in your brokenness, I feel safe enough to reveal a bit of my own, and before you know it, we slip our masks aside and see each other real face to real face."

–Linda Hoye

On Brokenness.

It's the middle of the night—3:00 a.m., to be precise—and I lay awake, tears streaking my face and dampening my pillow. "I'm not allowed to be broken," I whisper to myself.

There is nothing quite so harsh as the feeling that you cannot be what you so obviously are in that moment. When grief washes over you and waves of deep ache and loss are all you can fully feel. Yet, it's not acceptable to still feel this way or feel this way at all! It was okay for a little while when cancer had stolen my friend in the middle of a pandemic and the grief was obvious, expected, acceptable. But six months later, as I wrestled with other losses and complicated relationships and no one could see the cracks, I felt like I needed to be whole. Yet I still felt so broken. I began to avoid and narcotize. I avoided anything that caused me pain. I avoided my kids, my husband, other friends, and family. Relationships equalled pain, and I simply couldn't deal with any of it. I felt so broken. And yet completely unable to confide in anyone.

Our society has taught us that we need to be slaying and powering through constantly. And while there are times when this is entirely possible and true, we are so very human and need to take care of the beautiful, emotional soul within. When we feel grief and pain and even numbness, it's okay to take a moment and just let that feeling be. None of this "I should…"

crap.

Even Jesus felt overwhelmed by emotions at times and had to step away to be alone.

If you need to take a day, do it.

Take a full day to care for yourself. For some people, it may take a hike in the mountains or kayaking or skiing. For some of us, it's a hot Americano by a crackling fire with a cozy sweater and a book. It may be spending time in prayer, doing yoga, or running ten kilometres. It may be tucking yourself back in under the covers and getting some much-needed sleep.

The point is, we are human and cannot keep a perfect mask on indefinitely.

We all have a breaking point, and it's healthy to recognize the signs and defuse that bomb before it goes off.

"The great thing about getting older is that you don't lose all the other ages you've been."

—Madeleine L'Engle

On Milestones.

As I'm finishing up the first draft of this book, my 40th birthday is less than a week away. My goal was to have the finished copy in my hand by this date. I like my numbers neat and tidy, and it would have been, well, perfect. But along the way, I had to let go of that idea. I wanted a book that wasn't rushed, that I didn't just slap together so that I had something out in the world on a specific date. I wanted to leave the world with a labour of love.

And that's 100% what this is.

I often set lofty goals that are hard, if not impossible, to achieve. In my thirties, I created a bucket list of all the things I wanted to accomplish before I hit 40. I called it my 40 Before 40, and there were some Big Dreams on there. I accomplished a few on the list: visit Italy, find a good therapist, go on a cruise, read 100 books. But many more remain unaccomplished: visit 10 countries, go skydiving, run a half marathon. I have no doubt I can still accomplish these things. But a few years in, I realized that it didn't need to be things that I accomplished but desired emotions.

This bucket list of feelings could include items such as alive, vibrant, serene, victorious, content, accomplished... these are emotions that can be felt in a variety of different circumstances. Some of my previous bucket-list ideas might create these feelings, but switching the focus from the "doing" to the "feeling" is a lot more powerful. I can cross all these big items off a list, but if that's all I'm doing it for, where's the value? I want to live fully, joyfully, present, and alive.

It feels like 40 is a great time to start. Maybe you've started already, awesome!

Maybe you feel it's too late; I promise you, it's not. Choose today to live every moment completely engaged and alive.

I'm excited for 40. If that makes me strange, I'm okay with that! I loved turning 30, and I feel like I have so much more wisdom that I've picked up from difficult and powerful experiences. I would never choose to go back to any point in my life... it's been a great life, but I don't need to relive any of those lessons. I look forward with joy and anticipation for what's ahead. It can only get better as I lean on Jesus and stand on his promises. I have the best people surrounding me, and I'm committed to lifelong learning and growth.

If I could leave some advice for my younger self, it would be this:

- Live in the moment without trying to control every aspect. So much energy can be wasted on controlling how things turn out. I would tell myself to chill a lot more.
- Pick your battles because the little things don't really matter in the long run. If you were living to the fullest, sharing your joy and creativity with the world, it doesn't matter what you wore or how you carried those extra pounds. What matters is how you made others feel.
- Show compassion to yourself especially, and then to others. It's easy to find fault in others, to point fingers and place blame, but it's even easier to do this to yourself. And I want to remind you, you were made by God in His perfect image. And God doesn't make mistakes.
- Keep going. You're rarely going to get it right on the first try. It'll be worth it if you just keep at it!

"We delight in the beauty of the butterfly, but rarely admit the changes it has gone through to achieve that beauty."

—Maya Angelou

On Moving Forward.

In closing, I want to leave you with practical ways to move past the damaging habits you've held on to for so long. I'm a visual person, so I took each lie, reversed it, wrote it in bold letters on a bright Post-it® note, and stuck it on my mirror or beside my laptop. My list looked like this:

My identity lies not in how I can impress the people in my world or how well I portray my life online. It lies not in how bright and white my shoes are and how carefully I need to tiptoe to keep them that way. My identity has absolutely nothing to do with my curated social grid or the filters I use.

My identity lies simply in this:

- I'm created to fill a place no one else can, to tell stories no one else can.
- I'm loved just the way I am, with my flaws, my tears, my exhaustion, and my impatience... and yet...
- I'm empowered to show up, to learn and grow, to not stay stuck.
- I'm forgiven for all the ways I've messed up and will continue to mess up until the day I leave this earth. It's all covered, by Jesus.

Remember, there is no one right way to do things, whether it's loading the dishwasher, raising kids, marriage, or even worship. We are all individual and unique and deeply loved by God. The parts of yourself you think are imperfect are the parts that draw people to you. All you need to do is embrace them and the truth that not one part of you is a flaw or a mistake.

This morning, like every morning, I went for a walk. It is one of those intensely perfect June days we live for all winter here on the Canadian prairies. I had my coffee in hand, still steaming hot in my engraved Yeti that states, "First the coffee, then the adventures." I walk with my 15- and 11-year-old boys, and I marvel that they both love my company. I hope that never changes. I walk across the highway with them and thank the faithful and friendly crossing guards. They keep my kids safe every day, rain or shine, blizzard or dry summer heat. I wave goodbye to my boys at the school and keep walking. I do my regular morning loop—I am a creature of habit, after all—and I take a right at the Y in the path instead of my usual left.

I keep walking, and I feel this overwhelming gratitude and contentment. This feeling comes more often these days. We're pulling through the pandemic, I'm pulling through the depression with meds and daily walks, we're pulling through the marriage and parenting with grace and hard conversations, we're pulling through the faith journey one step at a time, we're pulling through in business with a dash of daring and determination.

I walk, and I feel like I might burst. This moment, this snapshot, this town, this body, this warm summer day with vibrant green grass and birds chirping and mowers growling and traffic humming... this, right here, right now, is just perfect.

You see, perfection isn't found externally.

You can fight and flee and flex your whole life and never see that what's right in front of you—within you—is absolute perfection. You can live to be 47 or 93 and not realize how very deeply loved and blessed and fully, intentionally *created* you are.

I want you to know that you have been wholly loved since before you were born.

You bring a unique element of light and vitality to your corner of the world. The world needs all of you, the real you, the you that doesn't concern yourself with perfect social media feeds or the approval of others.

So go be your authentic self.

Acknowledgements

Thank you.

I have dreamed of writing a book since I was six years old. I rarely believed that I could or would. I want to thank Lyndsie Barrie for planting the seed and watering it, for giving me that push (or 10!) to finally start writing and call my myself an author without cringing. Thank you.

To my kids—Blake, Nick, Sawyer, and Ellie—who put up with all my distractions and gazing off into space in the middle of a question, thank you. You stepped up to the plate to cook meals, to clean toilets, and to do laundry. You are the most amazing kids I could have ever asked for, and I'm grateful!

Writing a book takes a ton of time and emotional space. I'm so grateful for the unwavering support of my husband who sent me daily words of encouragement and gratitude during some of the most challenging days. Thank you for being my rock and for picking me to do forever with. I love you.

Huge thanks to my editor, Chrissy Wolfe, who gently but honestly picked apart my entire manuscript and then gave me the blueprints to put it back together. Your input was invaluable, and this book would not exist in the world without your help.

Thank you to my parents who raised me in a secure and loving home. Thank you for teaching me about Jesus and showing me the value of hard work, honesty, and integrity. I would not be the person I am today without your love and guidance in my early years.

Manufactured by Amazon.ca
Bolton, ON